Bengal Cats

by Grace Hansen

Abdo CATS Kids

abdopublishing.com

Published by Abdo Kids, a division of ABDO, P.O. Box 398166, Minneapolis, Minnesota 55439.

Printed in China

102016

012017

THIS BOOK CONTAINS RECYCLED MATERIALS

Photo Credits: Depositphotos Enterprise, iStock, Shutterstock, Thinkstock

Production Contributors: Teddy Borth, Jennie Forsberg, Grace Hansen

Design Contributors: Dorothy Toth, Laura Mitchell

Publisher's Cataloging in Publication Data

Names: Hansen, Grace, author.

Title: Bengal cats / by Grace Hansen.

Description: Minneapolis, Minnesota : Abdo Kids, 2017 | Series: Cats. Set 2 | Includes bibliographical references and index.

Identifiers: LCCN 2016944152 | ISBN 9781680809190 (lib. bdg.) | ISBN 9781680796292 (ebook) | ISBN 9781680796964 (Read-to-me ebook)

Subjects: LCSH: Bengal cats--Juvenile literature.

Classification: DDC 636.8/22--dc23

LC record available at http://lccn.loc.gov/2016944152

Table of Contents

Bengal Cats

Bengal cats look like they belong in the wild! But they are true **domestic** cats.

Bengal cats come in many colors. Most are snow, brown, or silver.

brown

silver

snow

A **patterned** coat gives this cat its **unique** look. Some Bengals have rosette markings. Others have a marble pattern.

rosette

marble

Bengal cats have large oval eyes. They can be shades of blue, green, gold, or **hazel**. Their ears are rounded at the tips.

Bengals are larger cats.

Females usually weigh 8 to 12 pounds (3.6 to 5.4 kg).

Males can weigh up to 15 pounds (6.8 kg).

Bengals have **sleek**, strong bodies. Their hind legs are longer than their front legs. This helps them to jump high.

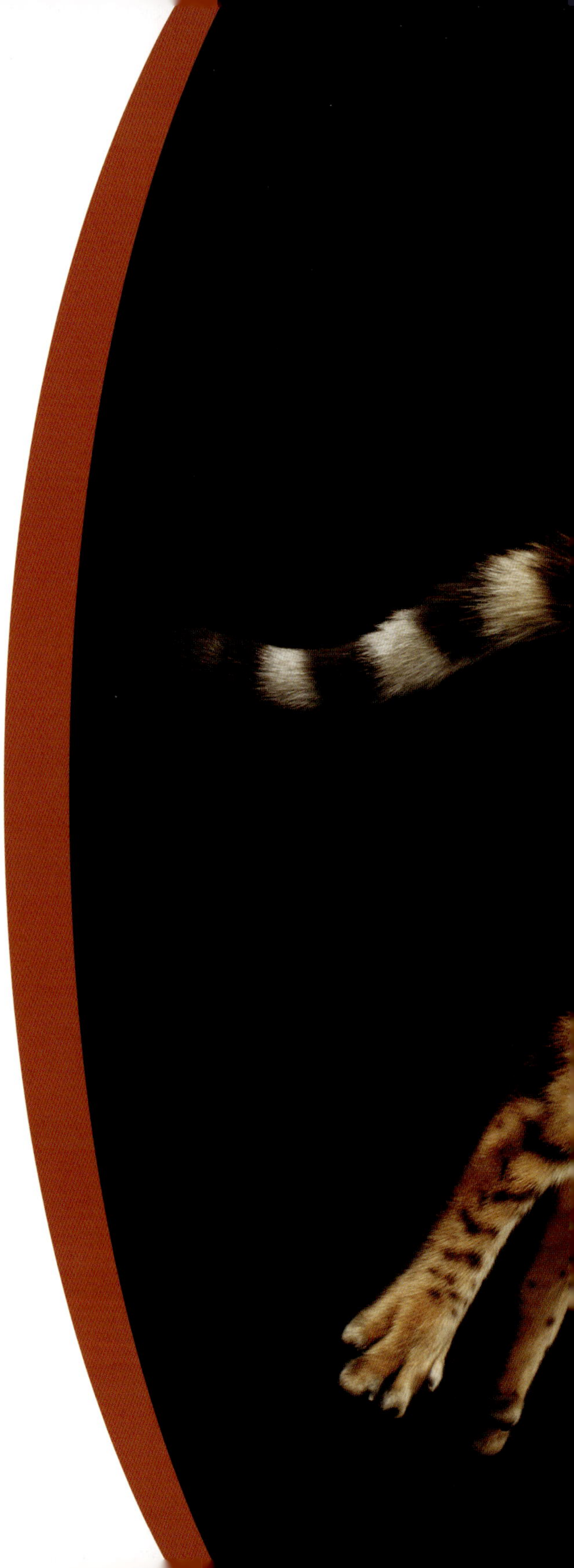

Grooming

Bengals are great at **grooming** themselves! Still, they should be brushed once a week. This keeps their coats healthy.

Personality & Play

Bengals have lots of energy. They are also very smart. Cat toys keep them busy. But playtime with family is their favorite!

Bengals are loving and friendly. If they are not busy climbing or playing, they are happy to cuddle.

More Facts

- Bengal cats do not meow like most cats. Instead, they bark, chirp, squeak, and howl.
- The Bengal cat was **bred** to have the beauty of a wild cat, but the personality of a **domestic** cat.
- Unlike most cats, Bengal cats love the water. They get this trait from their wild **ancestor** the Asian leopard cat.

Glossary

ancestor – someone or something that lived years ago that is related to a certain person or animal living today.

bred – made to look and act a certain way.

domestic – tame.

grooming – to clean and care for.

hazel – a reddish-brown or greenish-brown color.

patterned – having a repeated marking.

sleek – trim and graceful.

unique – very special and unusual.

Index

abdokids.com

Use this code to log on to abdokids.com and access crafts, games, videos and more!